CLASSICAL GUITAR
MASTERPIECES

AN OUTSTANDING REPERTOIRE COLLECTION FOR SOLO GUITAR

AMSCO PUBLICATIONS
New York/London/Paris/Sydney/Copenhagen/Madrid

COVER PHOTOGRAPH BY RANDALL WALLACE
MUSIC SETTING BY SETON MUSIC GRAPHICS

THIS BOOK COPYRIGHT © 1999 BY AMSCO PUBLICATIONS,
A DIVISION OF MUSIC SALES CORPORATION, NEW YORK

ORDER NO. AM 961906
INTERNATIONAL STANDARD BOOK NUMBER: 0.8256.1778.2

EXCLUSIVE DISTRIBUTORS:
MUSIC SALES CORPORATION
257 PARK AVENUE SOUTH, NEW YORK, NY 10010 USA
MUSIC SALES LIMITED
8/9 FRITH STREET, LONDON W1V 5TZ ENGLAND
MUSIC SALES PTY. LIMITED
120 ROTHSCHILD STREET, ROSEBERY, SYDNEY, NSW 2018, AUSTRALIA

PRINTED IN THE UNITED STATES OF AMERICA BY
VICKS LITHOGRAPH AND PRINTING CORPORATION

Contents

Fantasia

Music by John Dowland
Transcription by R. Sainz de la Maza

Lento

6

8

Sonata in D major

Music by Mateo Albéniz
Transcription by Graciano Tarrago

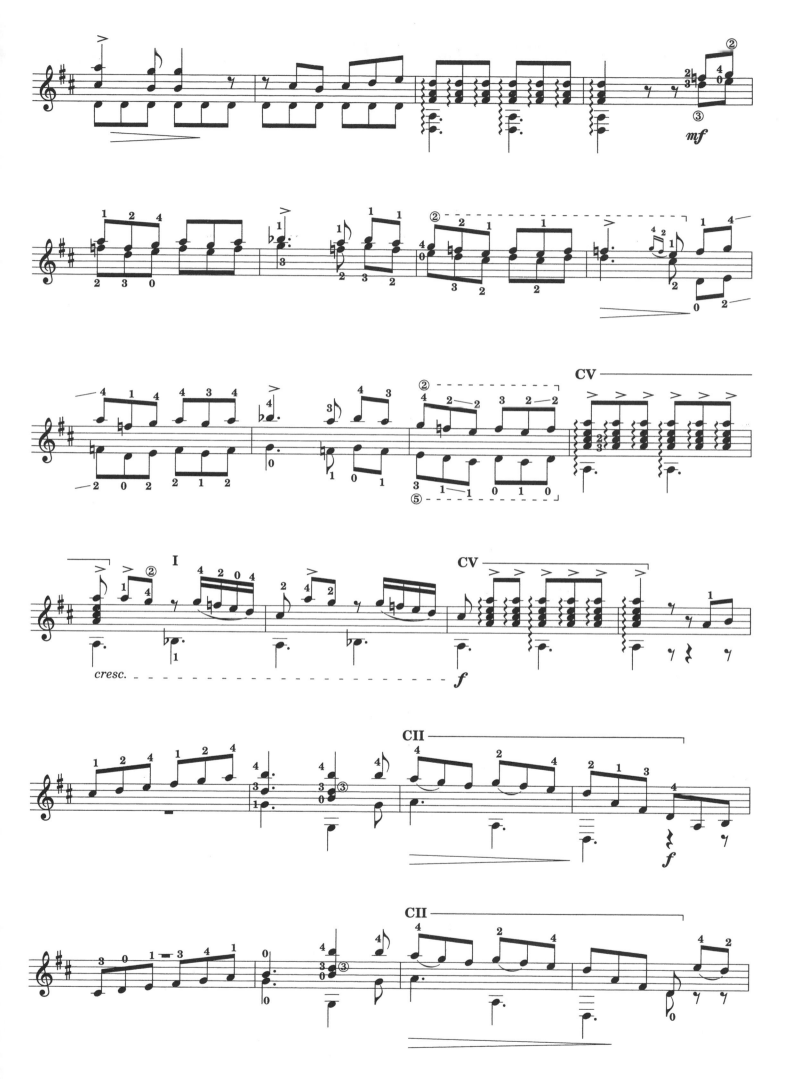

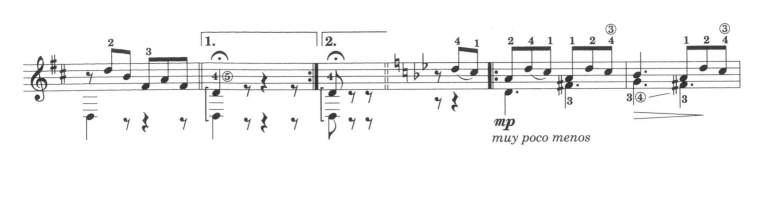

muy poco menos

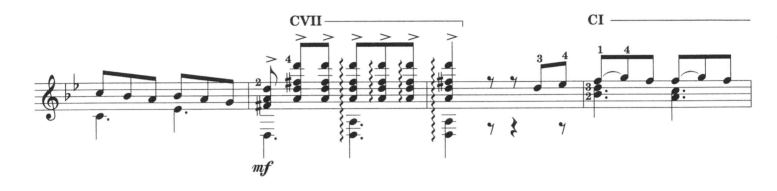

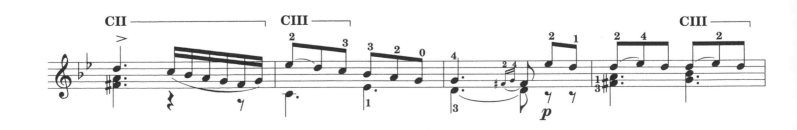

Canarios

Music by Gaspar Sanz
Transcription by Graciano Tarrago

Dance of the Miller

from The Three-Cornered Hat

Music by Manuel de Falla
Transcription by Siegfried Behrend

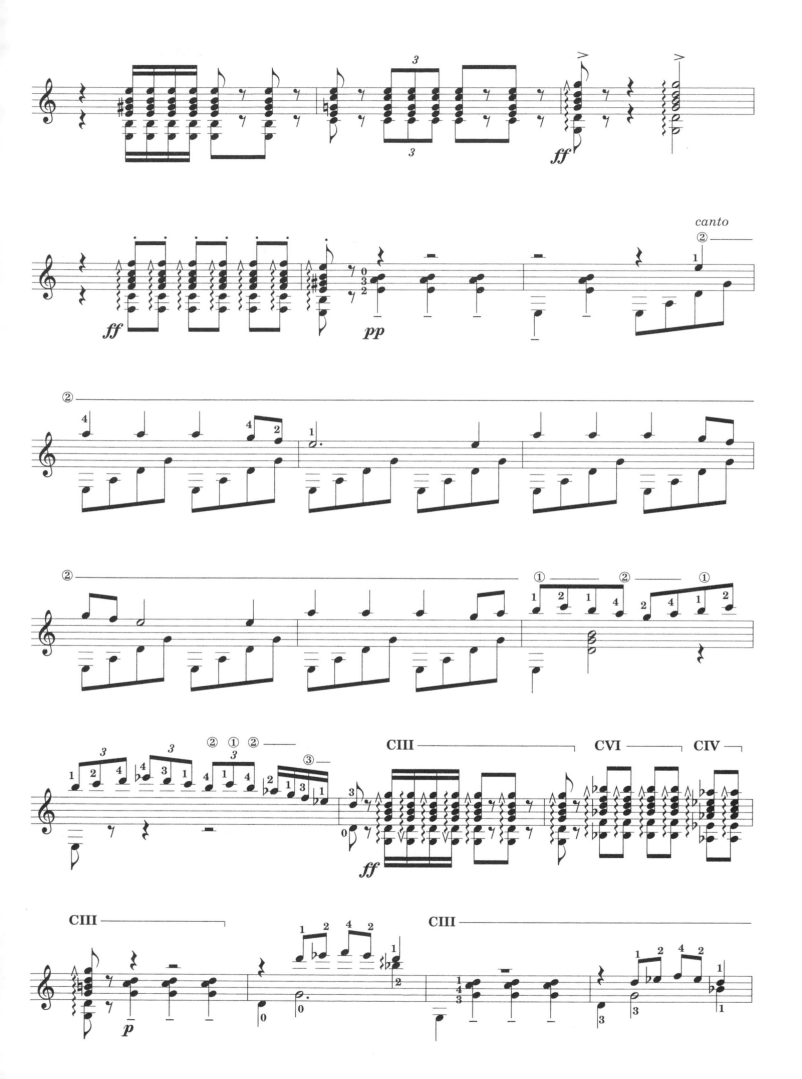

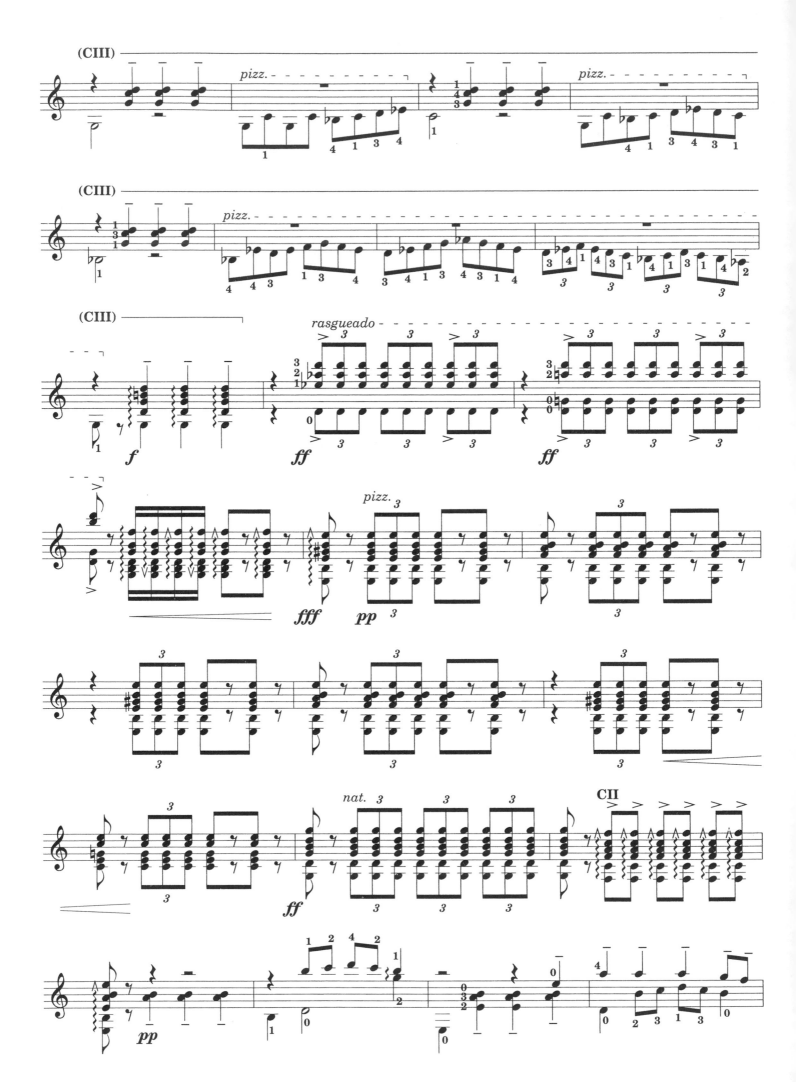

Recuerdos de la Alhambra

By Francisco Tarrega

Andante

Francisco Tárrega

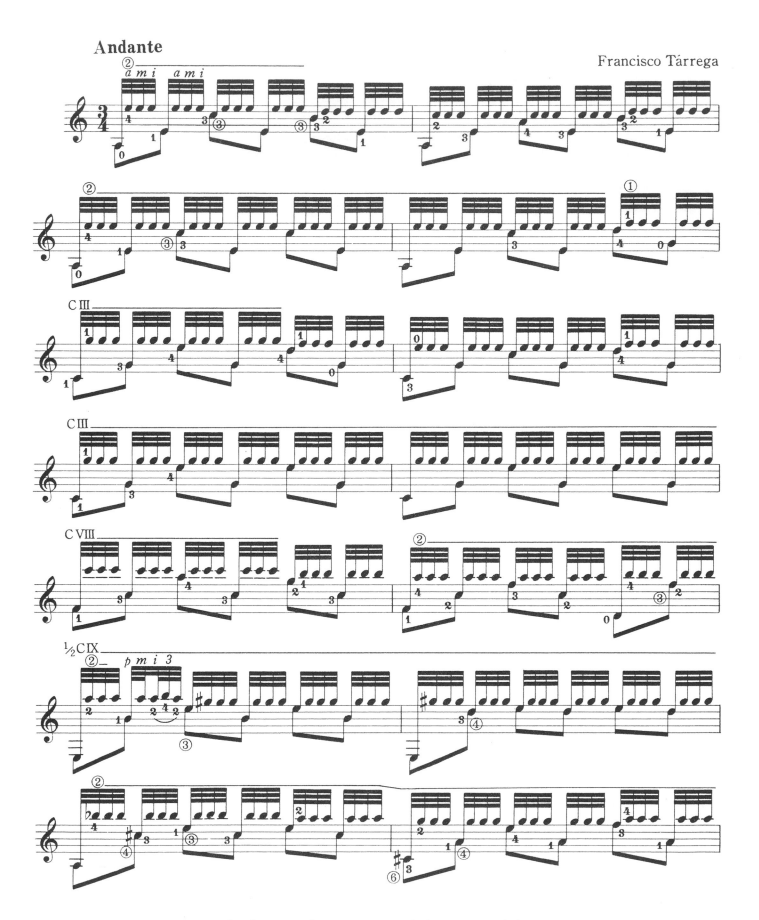

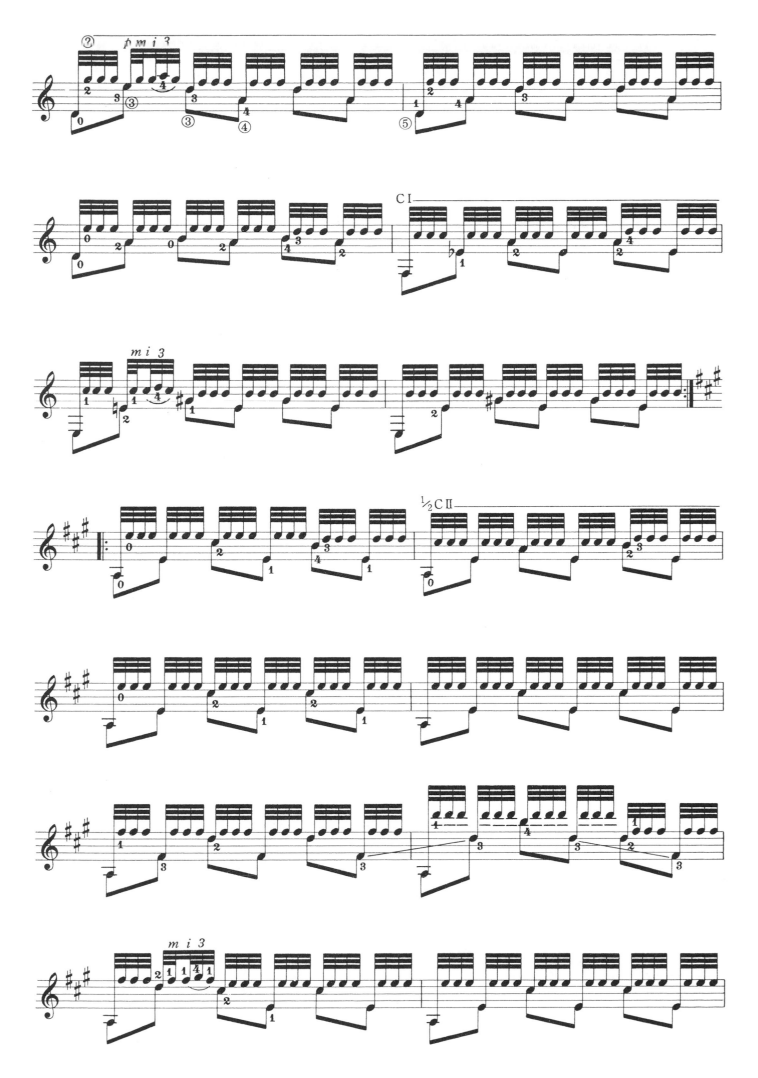

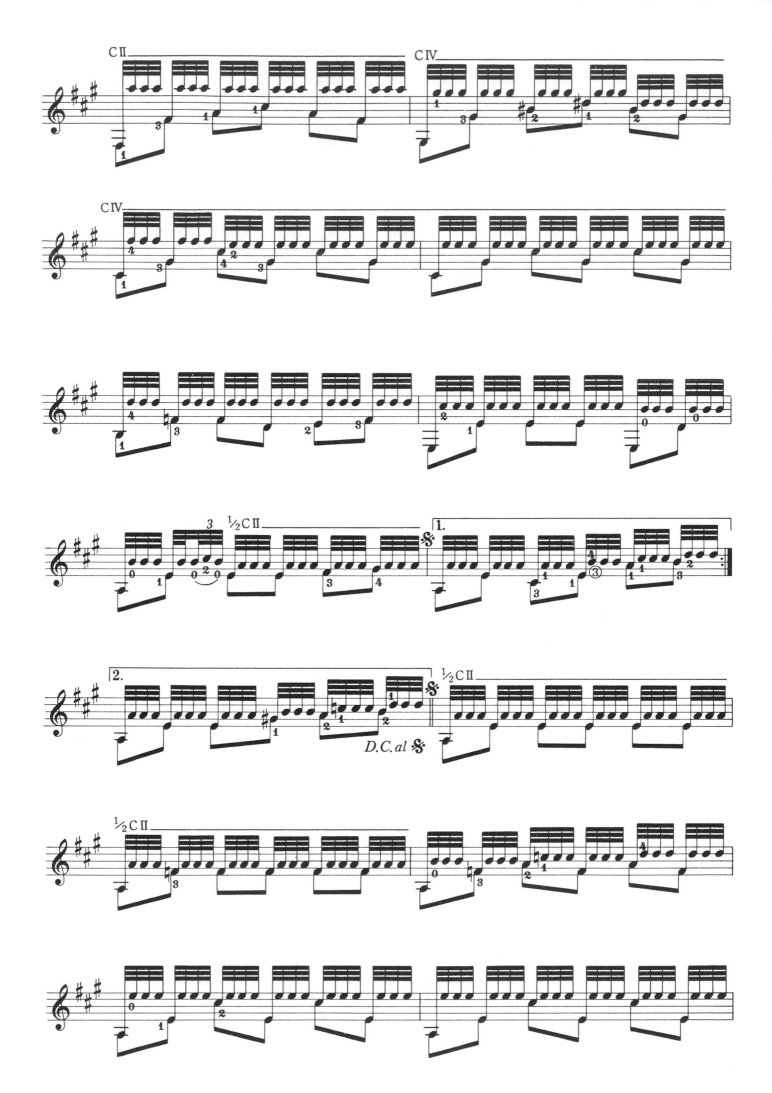

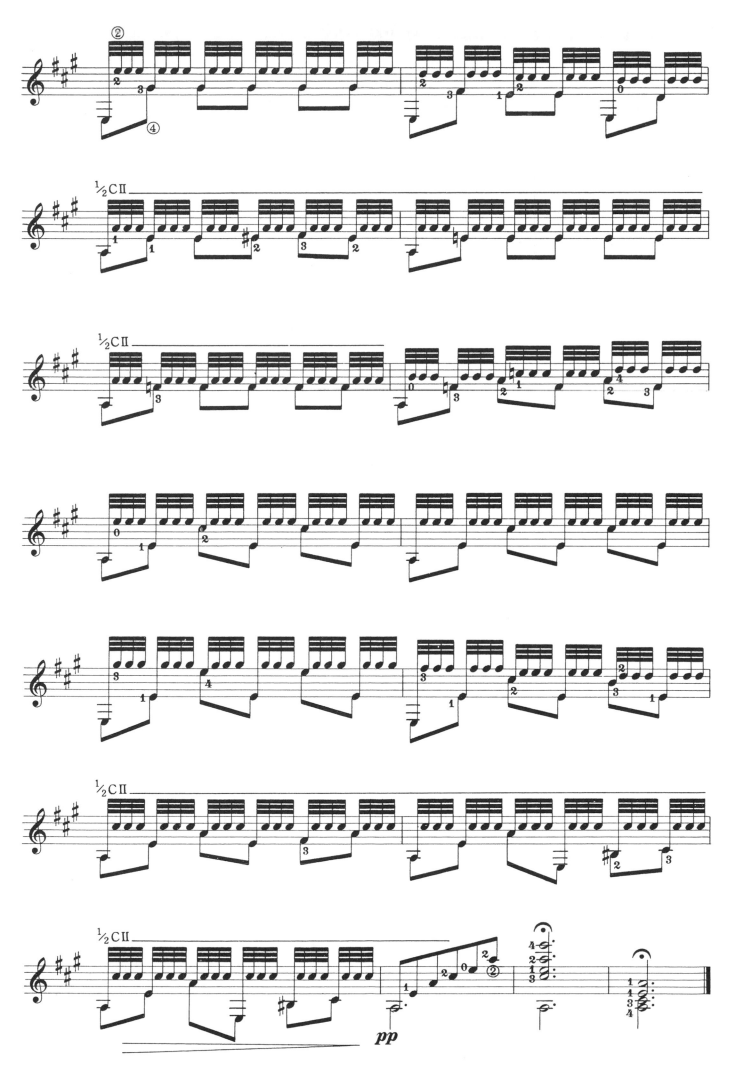

Mallorca
Barcarola

Music by Isaac Albéniz
Transcription by Luis Maravilla & Luis Lopez Tejera

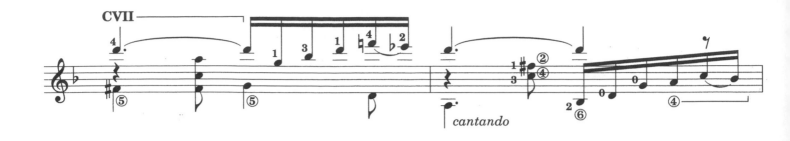

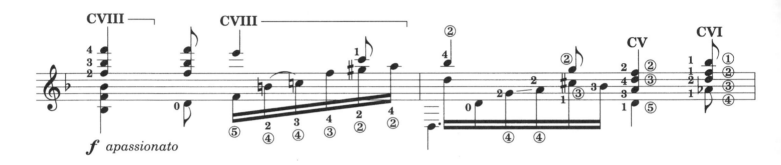

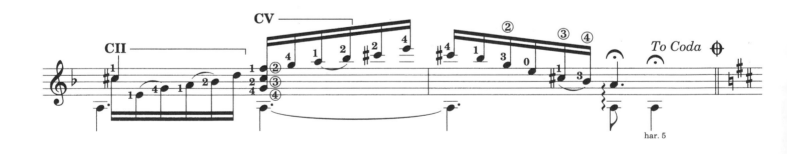

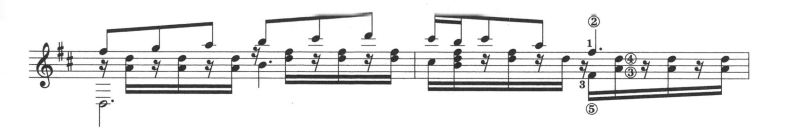

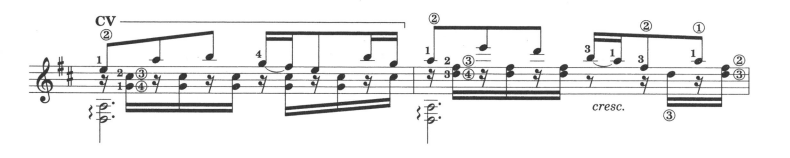

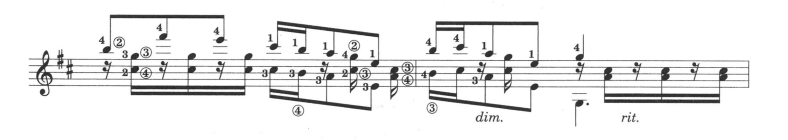

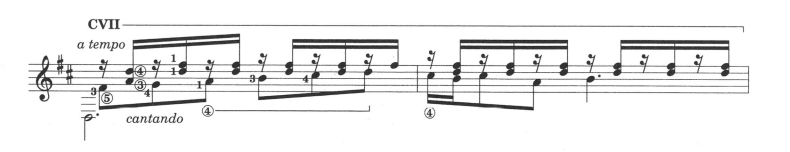

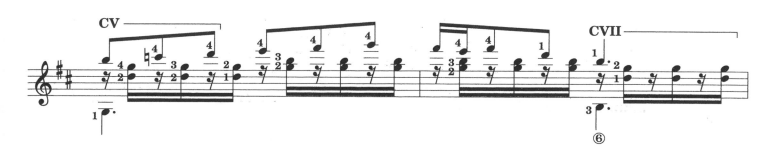

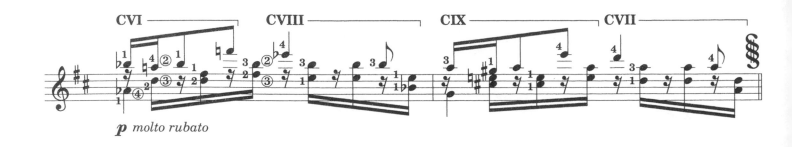

p molto rubato

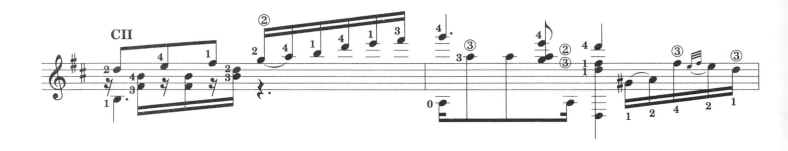

a tempo

cantando e dolce

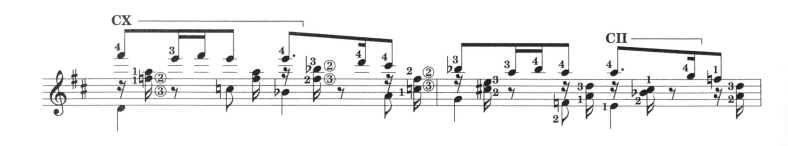

rit. molto

rit. e dim.

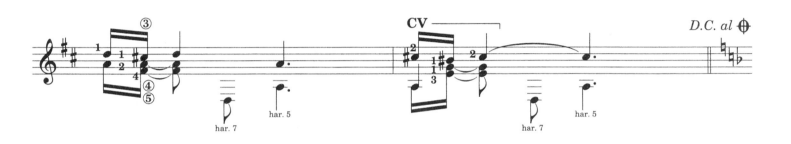

Coda

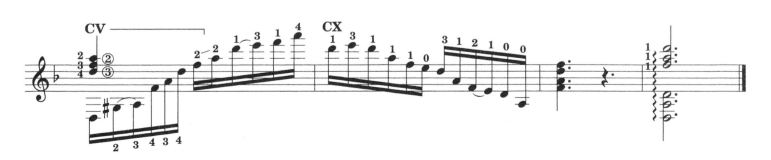

Granada (Serenata)
from Suite Española

Music by Isaac Albéniz
Transcription by F. Tarrega

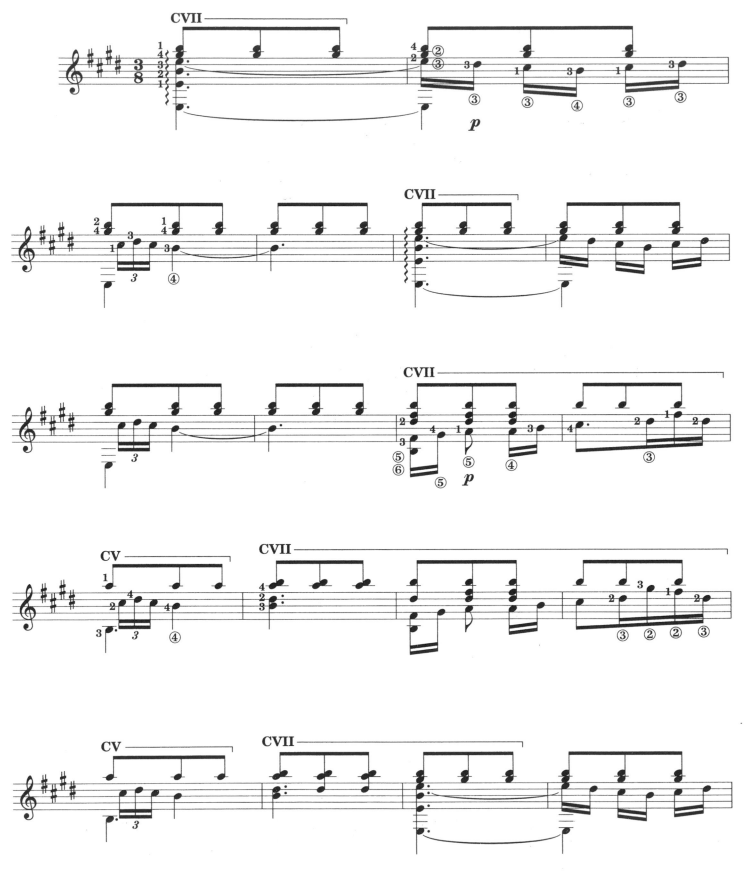

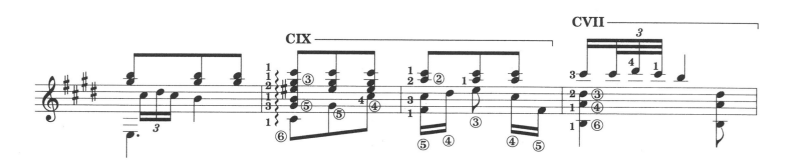

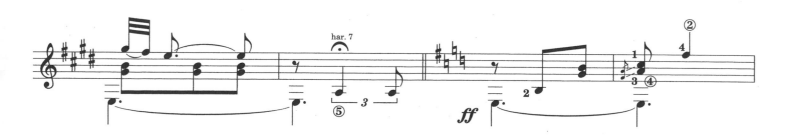

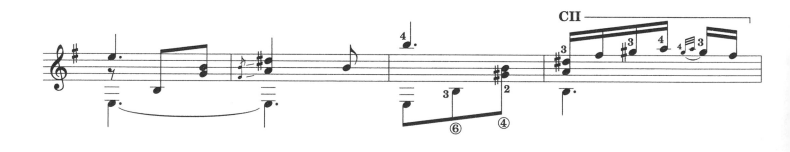

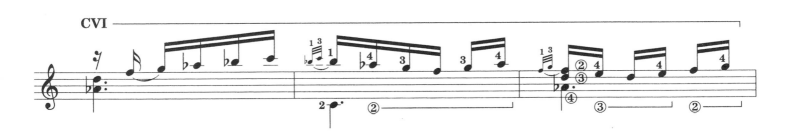

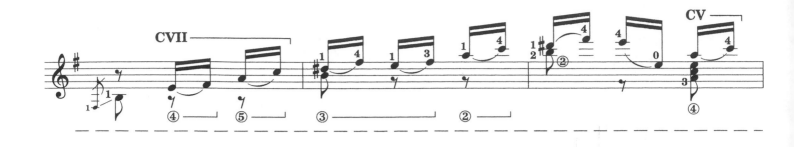

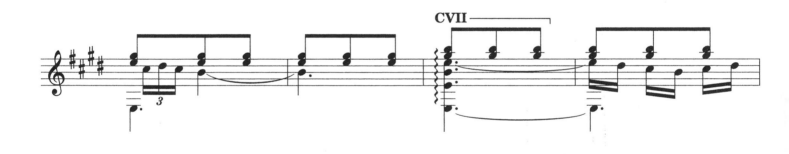

Cataluna (Corranda)
from Suite Española

Music by Isaac Albéniz
Transcription by V. García Velasco.

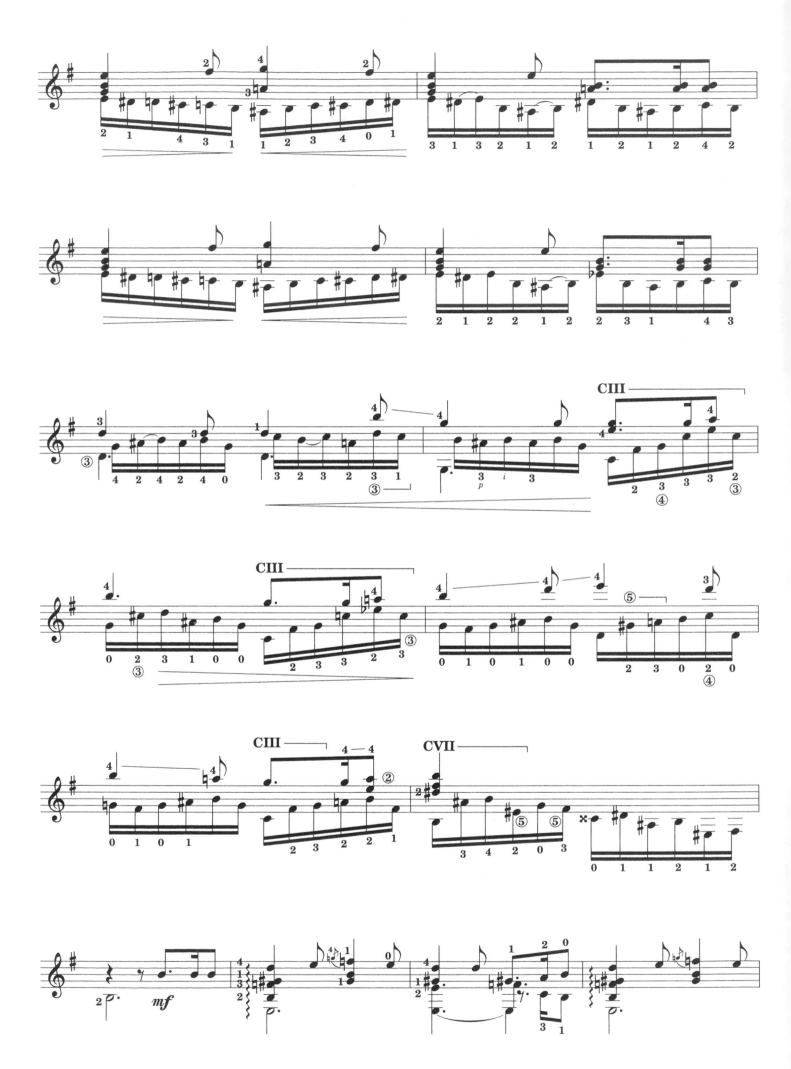

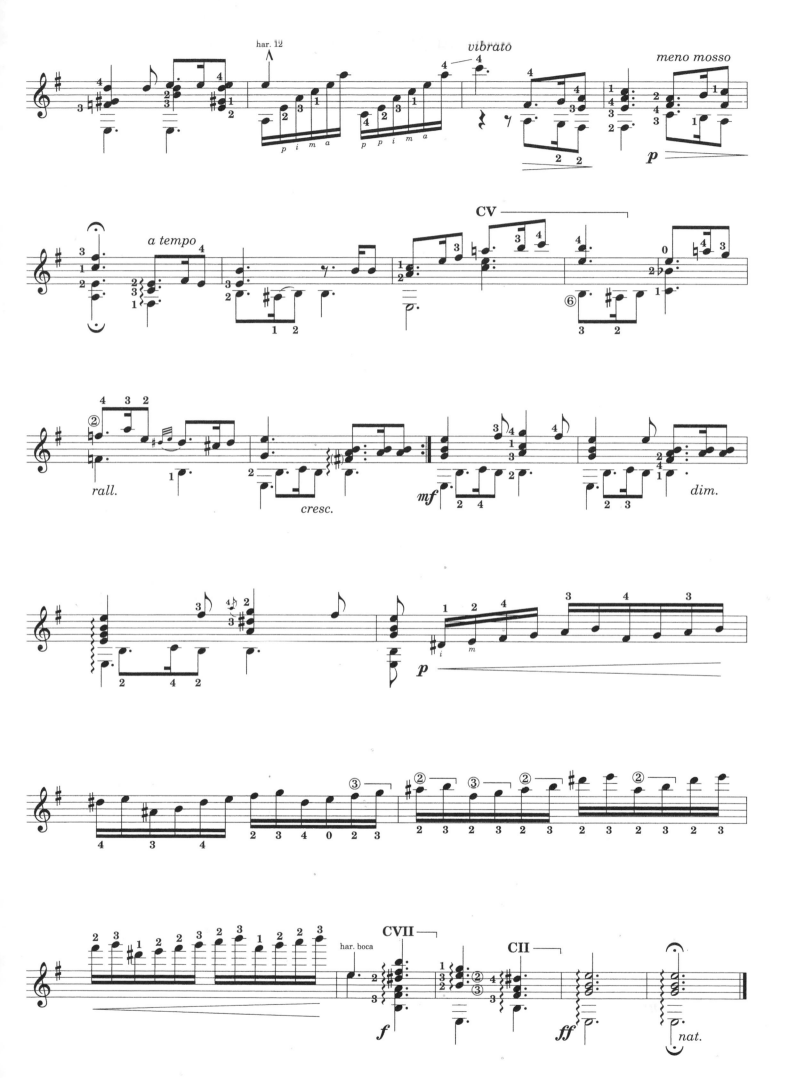

41

Sevilla (Sevillanas)
from Suite Española

Music by Isaac Albéniz
Transcription by F. Tarrega. Revised by Miguel Llobet

45

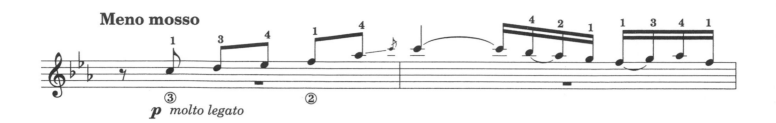

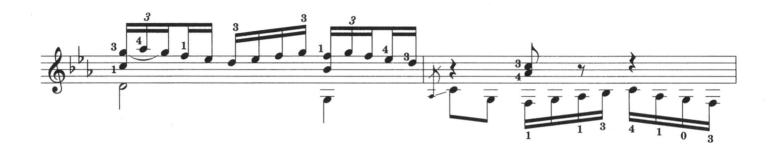

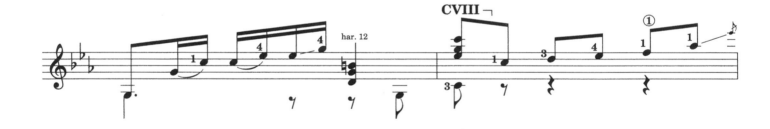

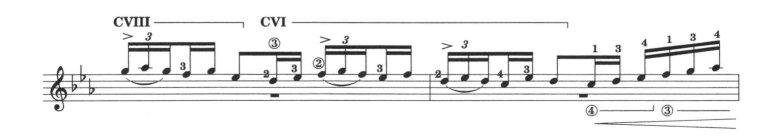

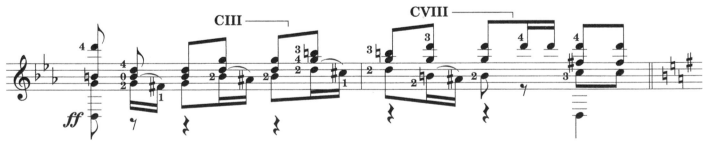

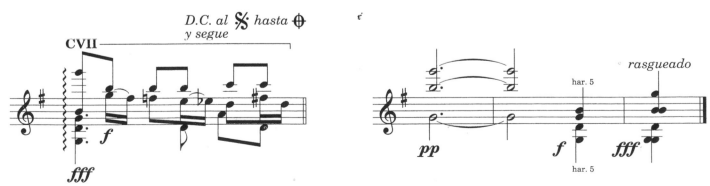

Cádiz
from Suite Española

Music by Isaac Albéniz
Transcription by F. Tarrega. Revised by Miguel Llobet

Allegretto ma non troppo

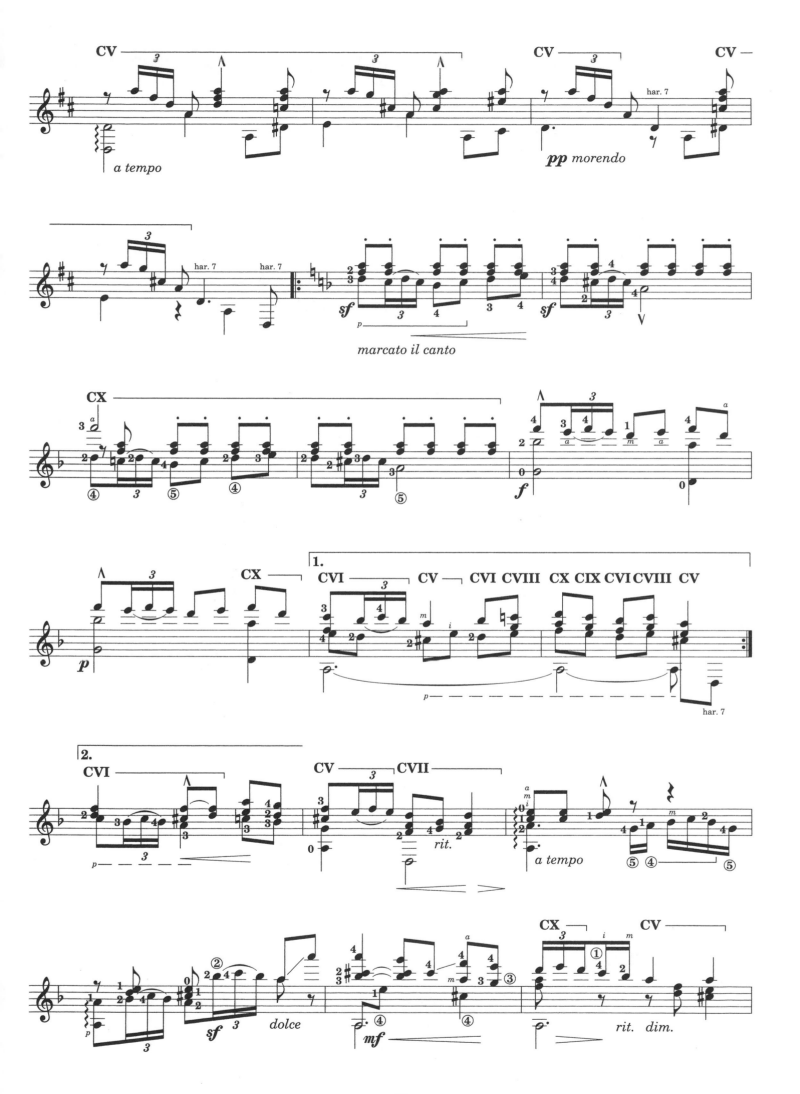

Leyenda (Asturias)
from Suite Española

Music by Isaac Albéniz
Transcription by Luis Maravilla

Allegro ma non troppo

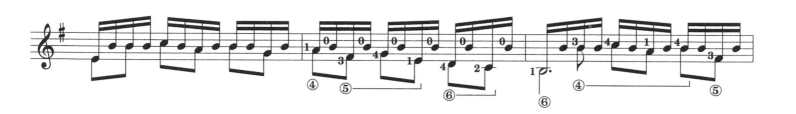

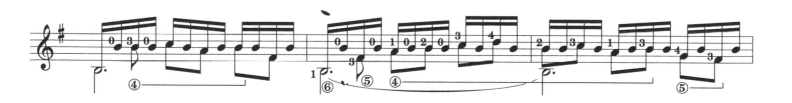

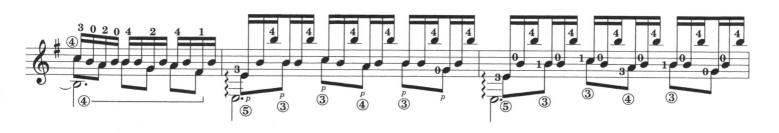

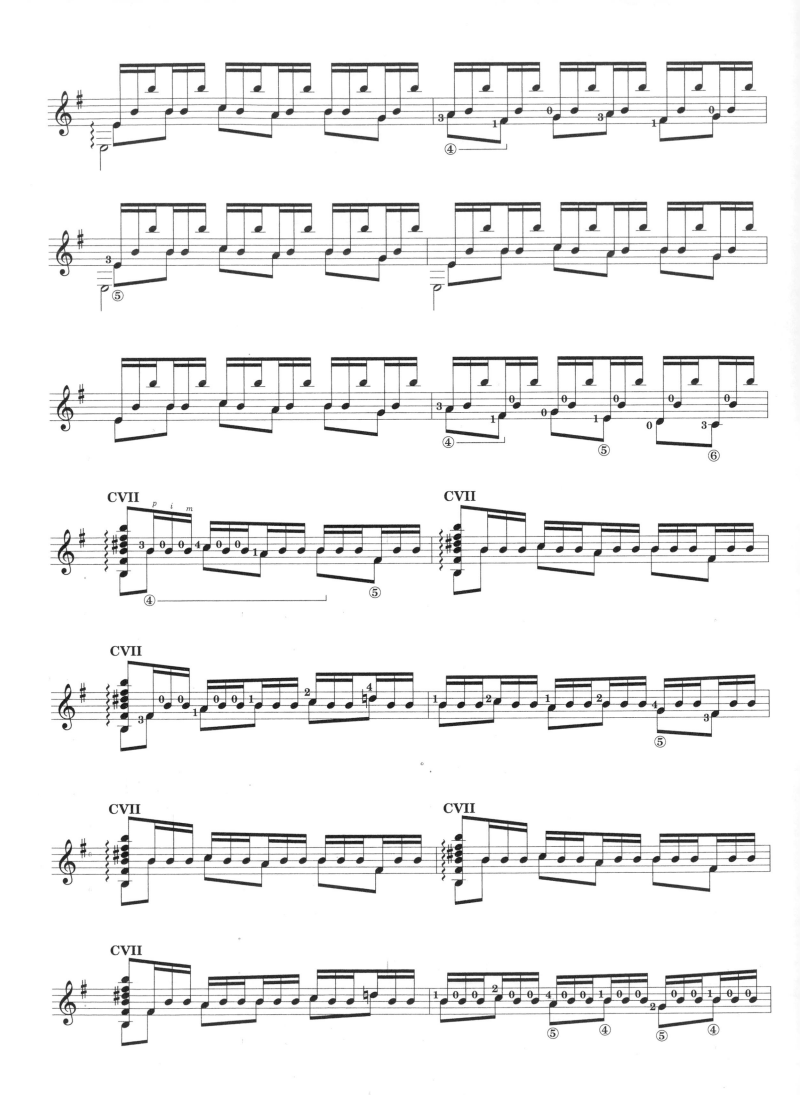

56

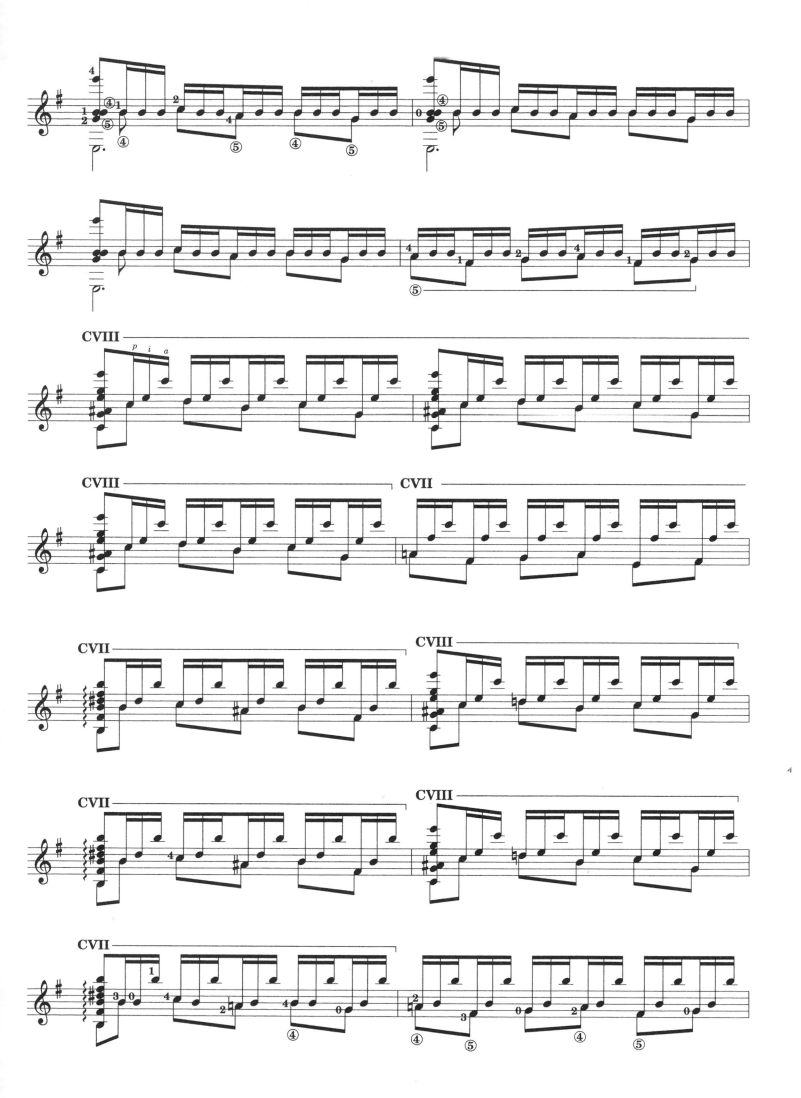

Cordoba
from Cantos de España

Music by Isaac Albéniz
Transcription by Ernesto Bitetti

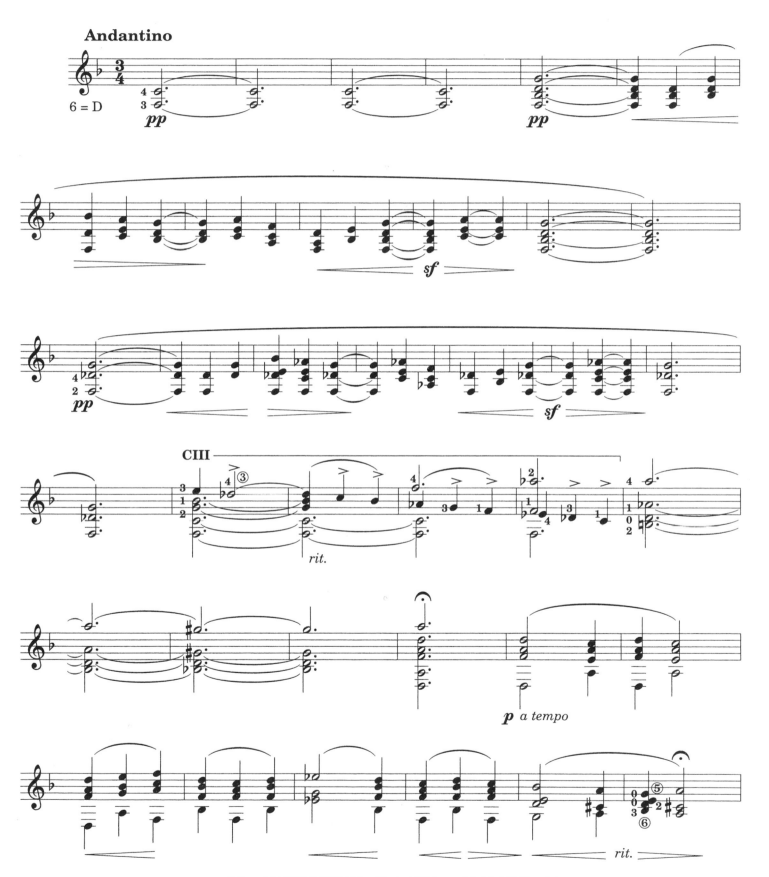

arpegiado abierto

66

Dedicatoria

From 'Cuentos de la Juventud'

Music by Enrique Granados
Transcription by Miguel Llobet

La Maja de Goya

Tonadilla

Music by Enrique Granados
Transcription by Miguel Llobet

Allegretto

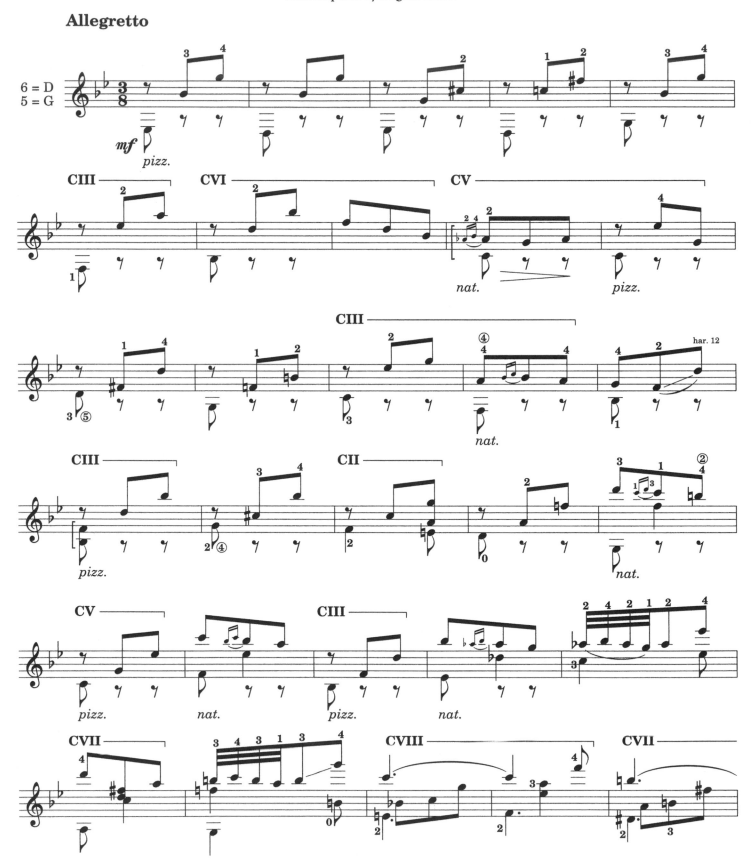

Greensleeves

Music by Francis Cutting
Transcription by Lupe de Azpiazu

1ª Volta = **Moderato espressivo**
2ª Volta = **Allegro spirituoso**

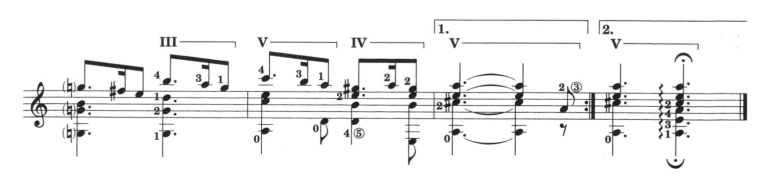

Danza Española No.4

Villanesca

Music by Enrique Granados
Transcription by José de Azpiazu

80

Andante espressivo

rit. molto e dim. pp

81

Danza Española No.5

Andaluza

Music by Enrique Granados
Transcription by Miguel Llobet

Andante – quasi Allegretto

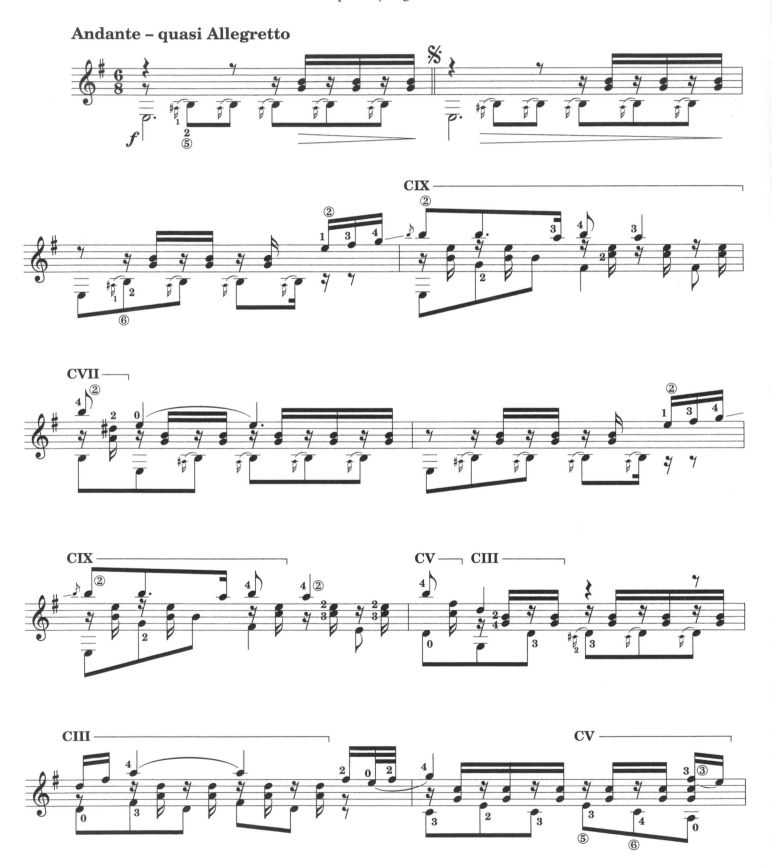

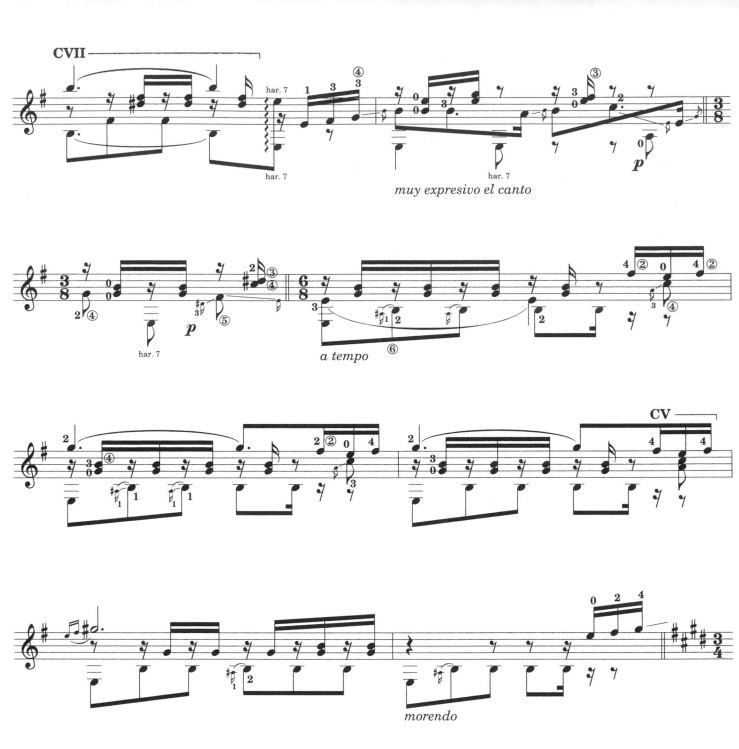

muy expresivo el canto

a tempo

CV

morendo

Andante

con molta expresion

poco *f*

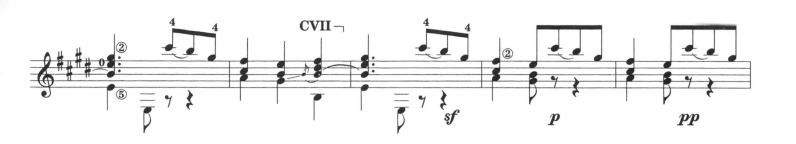

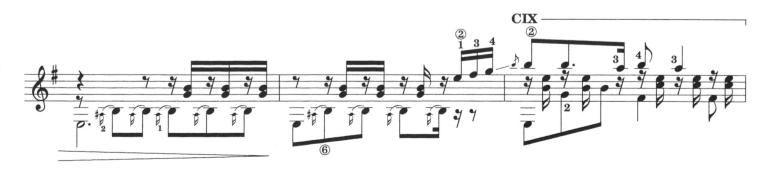

muy expresivo el canto

rit. molto morendo

Valses Poeticos

Music by Enrique Granados
Transcription by Rafael Balaguer

Introduction

1

91

2

Tempo de Vals noble

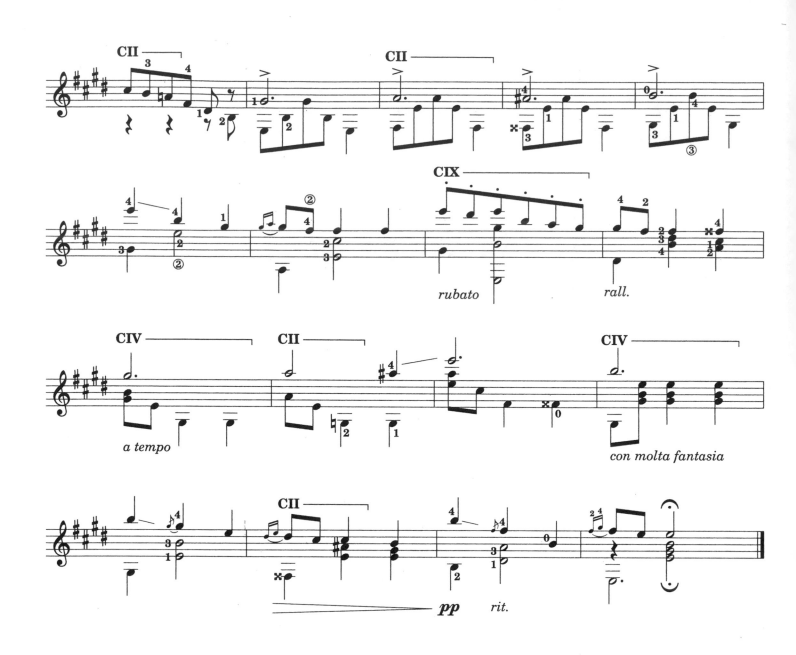

3

4

5

Allegretto (elegante)

6

Quasi ad libitum (sentimental)

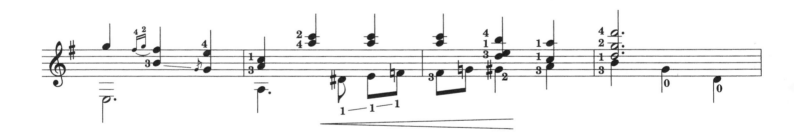

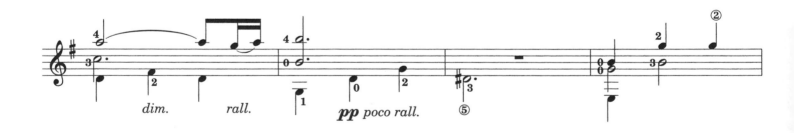

7

PRESTO

101

ADVANCED GUITAR MUSIC
from Music Sales

SONATINA Op.51
Lennox Berkeley CH01803

THEME AND VARIATIONS Op.77
Lennox Berkeley CH00480

HOMENAJE: LE TOMBEAU DE CLAUDE DEBUSSY
Manuel de Falla CH55674

MANUEL DE FALLA MUSIC FOR GUITAR
Arrangements of works from 'El Amor Brujo' and
'El Sombrero de tres picos' for guitar solo and duet.
CH61249

SONATA FOR GUITAR
Peter Maxwell Davies CH58941

SONATA GIOCOSA
Joaquín Rodrigo CH01807

THE CLASSIC GUITAR COLLECTION
Volume 1 AM32657
Solos from the fourteenth to twentieth centuries.
Including works by Bartók, Carcassi, Sor and Giuliani.

Volume 2 AM32665
A unique compilation of short pieces ranging from the
fourteenth century to Stravinsky and Shostakovich.

Volume 3 AM32673
Outstanding music for guitar players of all standards
including works by Bach, Mozart and Sor.

GUITAR MUSIC OF SPAIN
Volume 1 AM90240
Over 50 graded traditional pieces, by Bartolomé Calatayud.

Volume 2 AM90241
Compositions by Albéniz, transcribed for guitar.

Volume 3 AM90242
Traditional Spanish and hispanic music by composers such as
Rodrigo, Calatayud, Llobet, Cardoso, Sainz de la Maza and others.

THE RENAISSANCE GUITAR AM35882
THE BAROQUE GUITAR AM35890
THE CLASSICAL GUITAR AM35908
THE ROMANTIC GUITAR AM38993
Four centuries of solos, duets and songs for classical guitar and lute family.
Including fascinating background detail, fingering and playing tips.